Blue Zhejiang

Dr. Ocean Explores the Vertical Stratification of Marine Space

Written by

Wang Peng
Wu Jiexuan
Xie Fang
Yue Xihe
Guo Ziyan
Zheng Kaixuan

Translated by

Zhang Liyan

Books Beyond Boundaries

ROYAL COLLINS

Blue Zhejiang: Dr. Ocean Explores the Vertical Stratification of Marine Space

Written by: Wang Peng, Wu Jiexuan, Xie Fang, Yue Xihe, Guo Ziyan, and Zheng Kaixuan
Translated by: Zhang Liyan

First published in 2025 by Royal Collins Publishing Group Inc.
Groupe Publication Royal Collins Inc.
550-555 boul. René-Lévesque O Montréal (Québec) H2Z1B1 Canada

ISBN: 978-1-4878-1331-4

To find out more about our publications, please visit www.royalcollins.com.

Academician's Recommendation

The ocean is the cradle of life, a treasure trove of resources, the lifeline of transportation, and a strategic location. It is human's "second territory" and "blue granary" upon which we depend for survival. *Blue Zhejiang* is a popular science book written and illustrated by the team from the Marine Academy of Zhejiang Province, specifically for young readers. They have also produced a corresponding popular science video titled "Layer by Layer: Exploring Zhejiang." This book begins with the case of the multi-layered use of marine areas in Zhejiang, introducing the current challenges and potential solutions in marine space utilization. It employs vivid metaphors to explain the characteristics of marine spatial resources and presents an inspiring vision of the future world of vertically stratified marine utilization.

The three-dimensional utilization and high-standard protection of marine resources constitute a complex systematic project and represent a long-term scientific transformation process. Focusing on the ocean's goals of serving and integrating into the new development paradigm, this book introduces young readers the vertical marine usage and Zhejiang's approach toward marine spatial management through a combination of informative text and illustrations. It will help them understand both the current situation and long-term development, establish a sustainable development perspective, and become communicators and practitioners of "caring for the ocean, understanding the ocean, and developing strategies for the ocean."

MEMBER OF THE CHINESE ACADEMY OF ENGINEERING

DING DEWEN

Hello, everyone. I am Dr. Ocean. I'm engaged in research on the protection and utilization of marine resources. Over 70% of the Earth is covered by oceans, and the ocean and humanity are closely interconnected and influence each other.
The ocean is rich in resources, and the development and utilization of its marine resources can better achieve sustainable development for human society. Next, I will lead everyone to explore the "three-dimensional" ocean and embark on this wonderful journey!

In Ruian, Zhejiang Province, there is a unique marine area. Above the sea surface, a cross-sea bridge stands tall, providing convenience for transportation; beneath the surface lies an aquaculture farm; and on the seabed, cables for communication and power transmission run through. A three-dimensional development model has been realized in this single marine space, featuring "subsea communication, underwater production of green products, and surface transportation."

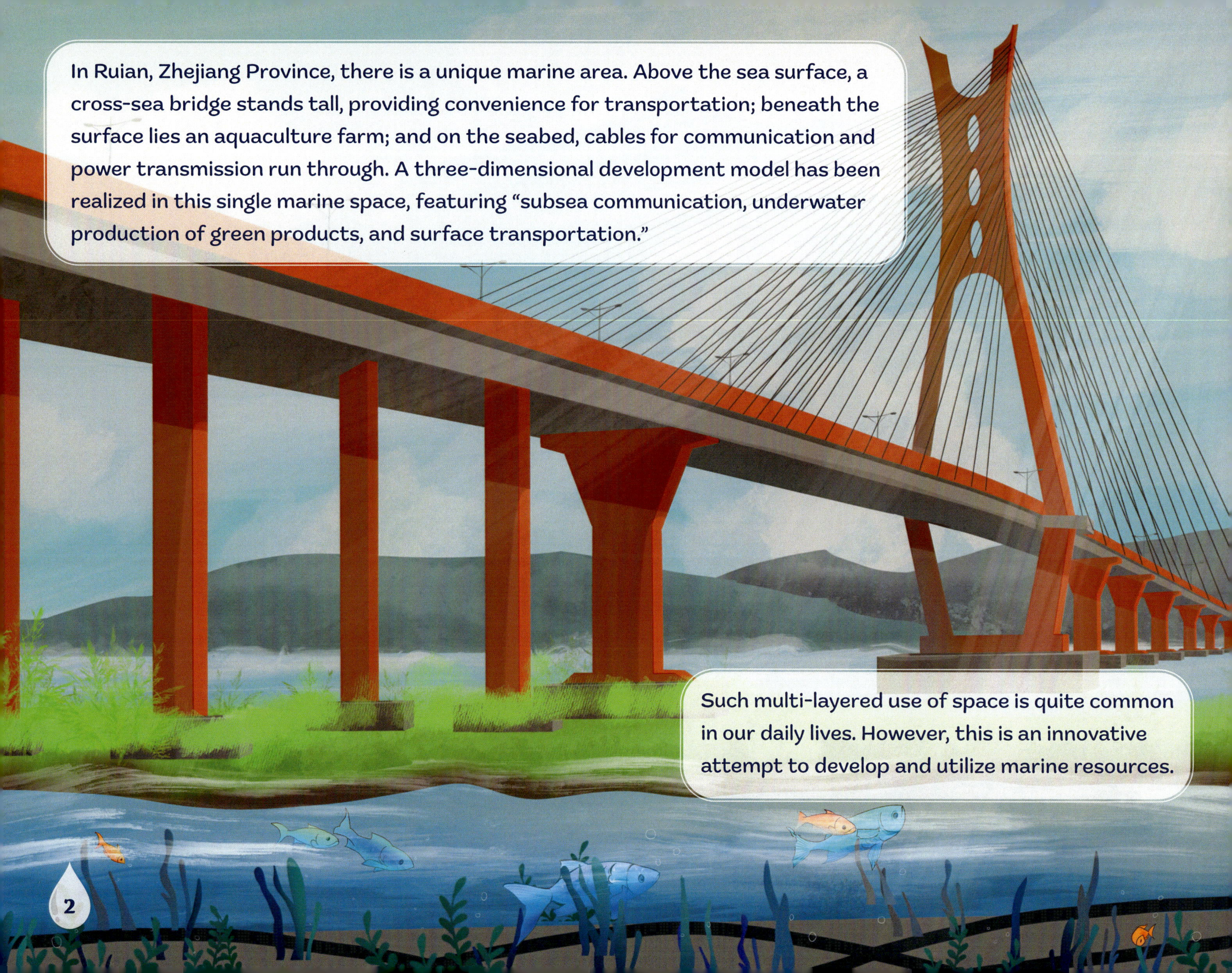

Such multi-layered use of space is quite common in our daily lives. However, this is an innovative attempt to develop and utilize marine resources.

In traditional marine development and utilization, managing and using marine resources often follows a relatively simple model, which views the ocean as a two-dimensional flat space. Under this model, a specific marine space is primarily allocated for a single purpose, such as fisheries, shipping, tourism, or energy development.

For example, if the sea area is used for aquaculture, the space above the sea surface and the seabed space are often left unused. Now, suppose there is a subsea cable that needs to pass through this area. Though it does not intersect with the aquacultural farm, it may lead to conflicts and contradictions regarding the rights to use the marine area.

The ocean covers a large portion of the Earth's surface, and its vastness often gives us the illusion that it possesses unlimited resources.

However, the nearshore areas closely connected to our daily lives and economic activities have undergone long-term development and utilization, and their high-quality spatial resources have become increasingly scarce.

With the fast development of science and technology and the growing demand for clean energy, emerging marine renewable energy projects such as offshore wind power, tidal energy, and wave energy are rapidly rising. These projects have a great demand for marine space, which spatially intersects and overlaps with that used for traditional marine industries such as fisheries, shipping, and tourism. Such multi-purpose demand for marine space has resulted in conflicts in resource allocation, and we must find an effective solution.

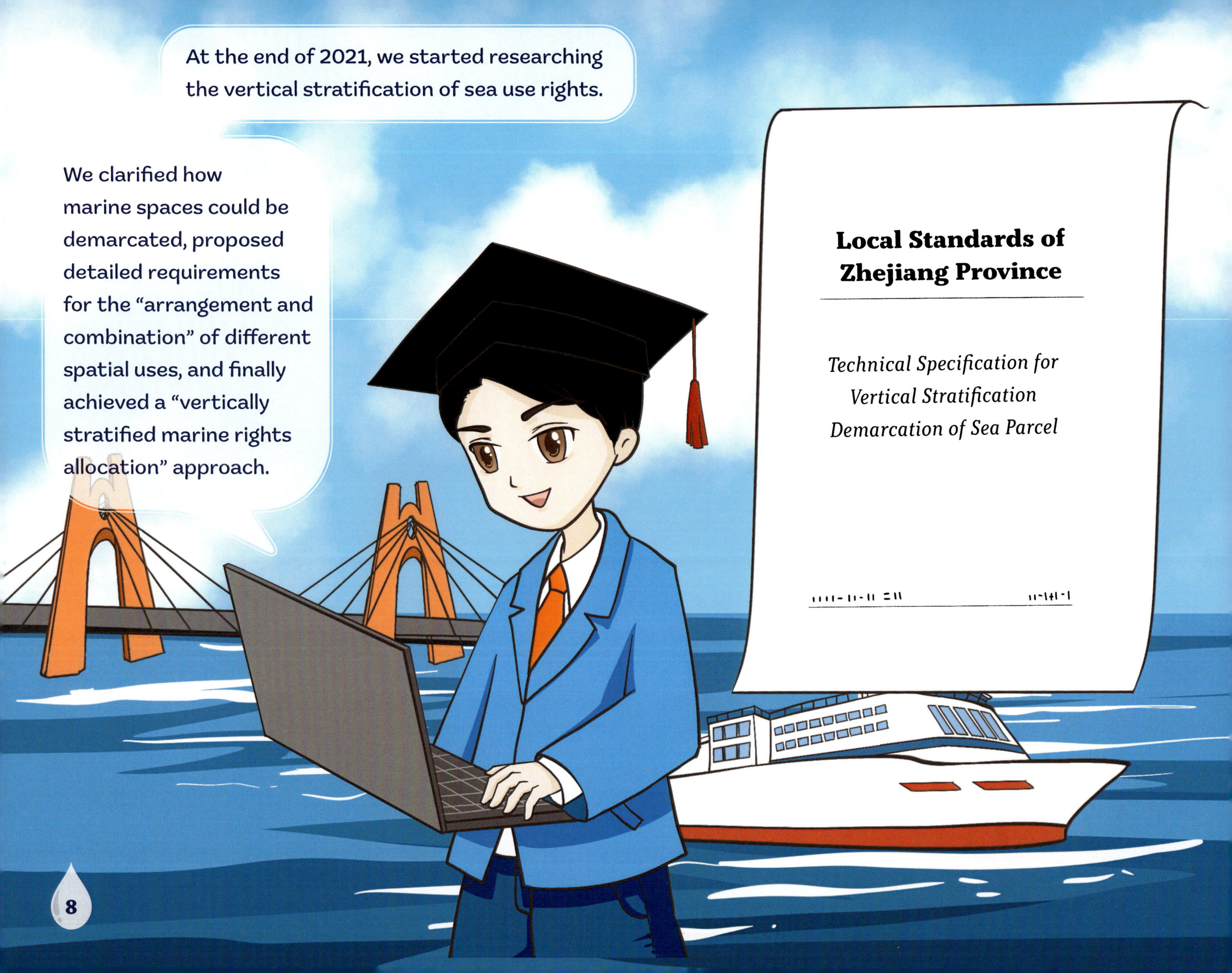
At the end of 2021, we started researching the vertical stratification of sea use rights.
We clarified how marine spaces could be demarcated, proposed detailed requirements for the "arrangement and combination" of different spatial uses, and finally achieved a "vertically stratified marine rights allocation" approach.
Local Standards of Zhejiang Province
Technical Specification for Vertical Stratification Demarcation of Sea Parcel

The ocean is a natural three-dimensional space.

What is achieved through vertical stratification of sea use rights is the transformation of this natural and vertical space into a managed three-dimensional space, allowing the sea area to become "three-dimensional" in terms of management.

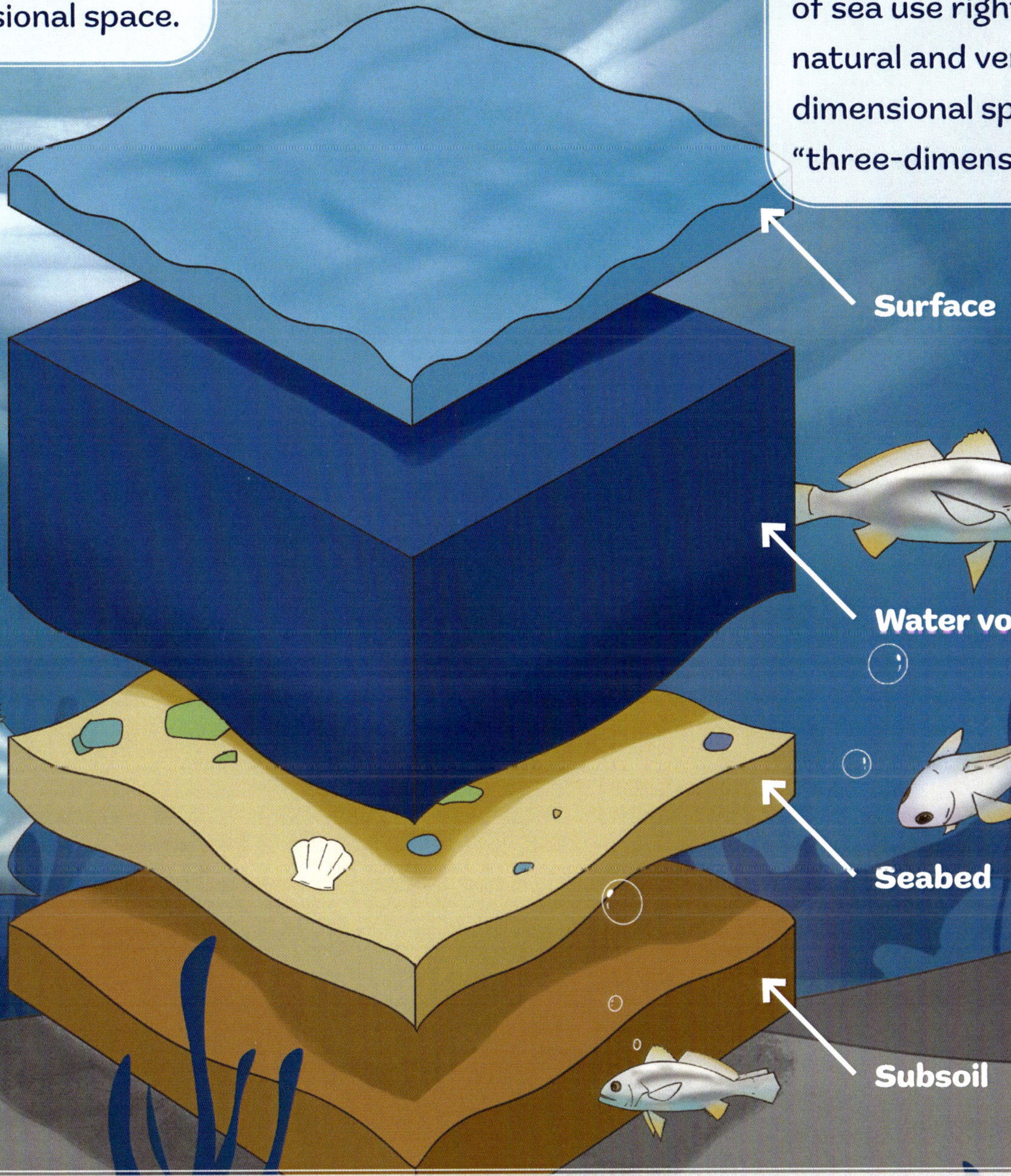

Based on current usage and management needs, we have divided the marine area into four layers: surface, water volume, seabed, and subsoil, with each layer having different resources and utilization methods.

We can compare the ocean to a water-filled plate to better understand this concept.

From the side view of the plate, the marine water surface is equivalent to the surface of the water in the plate, including the sea level and the space above it.

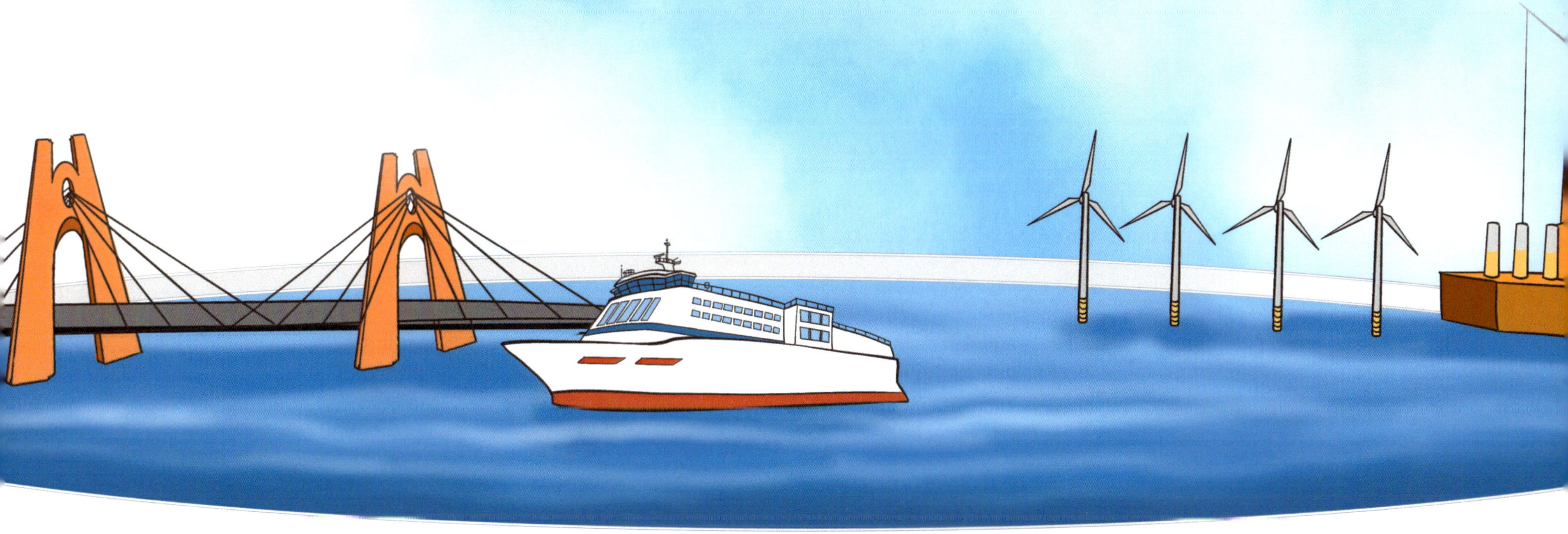

It is the birthplace of sea winds and waves and an ideal location for offshore wind power, ship navigation, and bridge construction.

Water volume
The marine water volume corresponds to the water within the plate, representing the space between the sea level and the seabed.

This layer is rich in biological and chemical resources and an excellent marine aquaculture site.

The seabed is equivalent to the bottom of the plate, vast and flat, which is also the surface of the seafloor, an ideal location for laying subsea cables and pipelines.

The subsoil is equivalent to the rim of the plate.

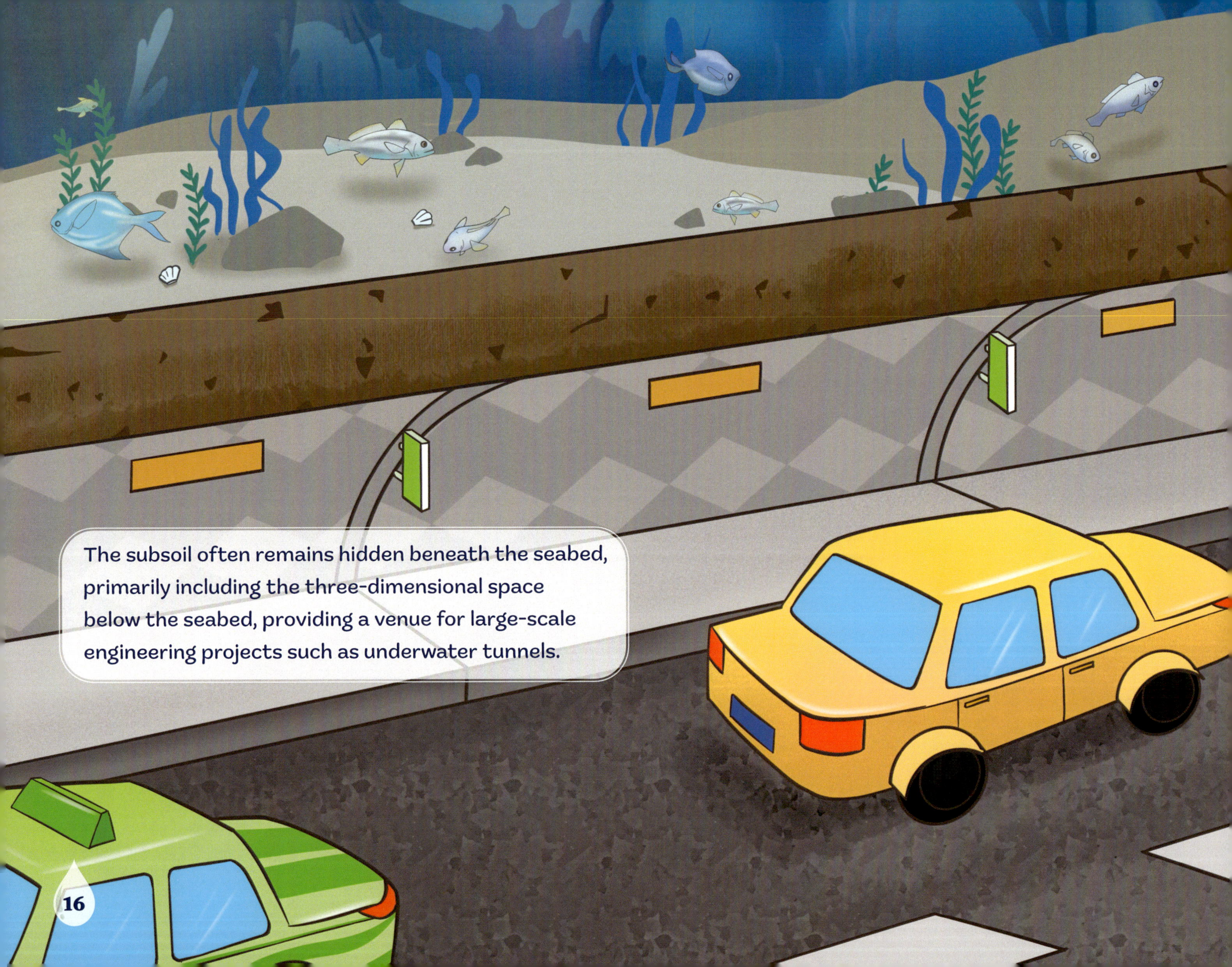

The subsoil often remains hidden beneath the seabed, primarily including the three-dimensional space below the seabed, providing a venue for large-scale engineering projects such as underwater tunnels.

Through scientific stratified management, the marine space for existing projects can be fully utilized while also opening new pathways for the "stacked" utilization of new projects.

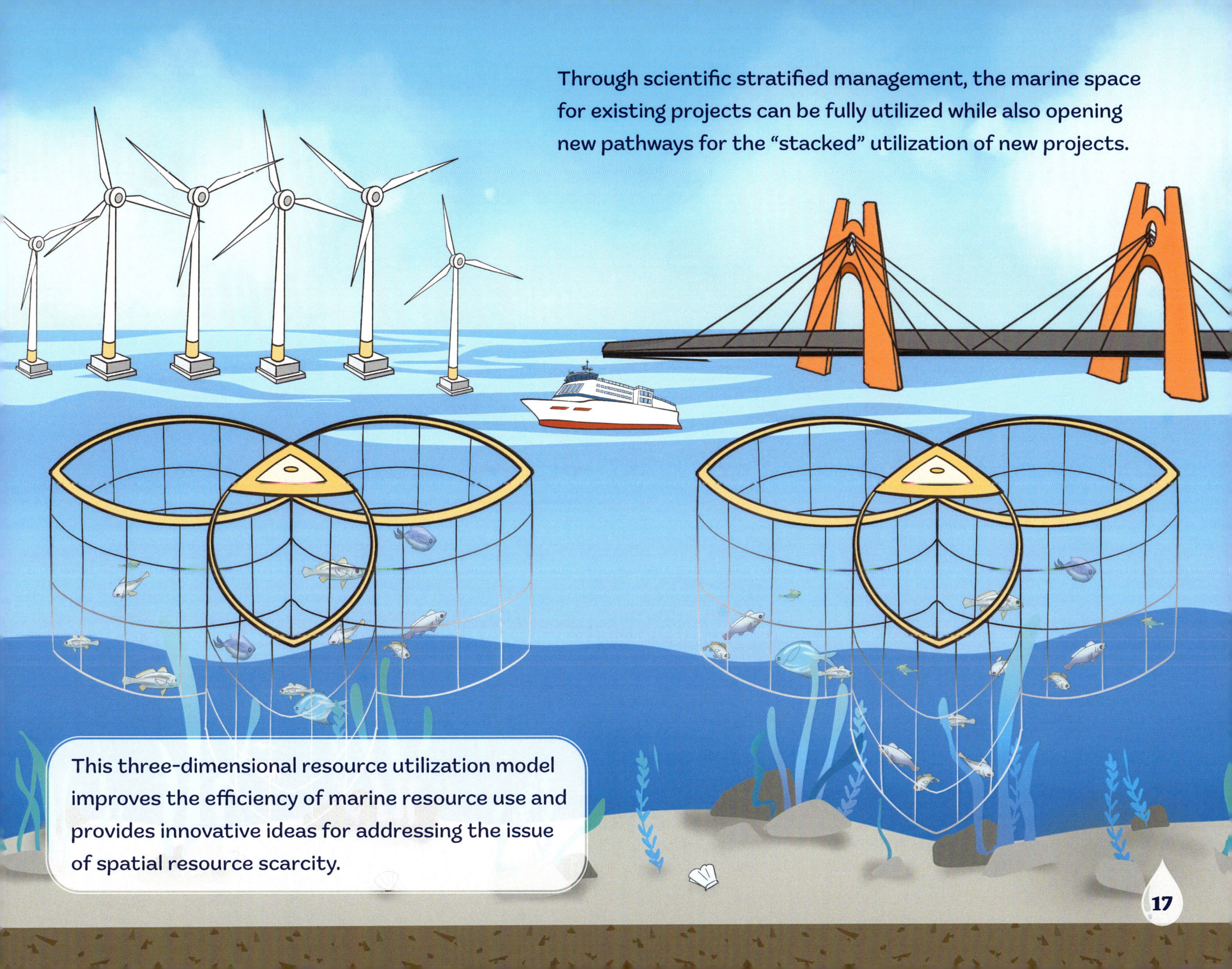

This three-dimensional resource utilization model improves the efficiency of marine resource use and provides innovative ideas for addressing the issue of spatial resource scarcity.

In the future, we will see a multi-dimensional and multi-functional marine utilization scenario.

Offshore wind farms and solar power installations will become important sources of clean energy above the water surface, providing stable, eco-friendly electricity for coastal cities.

Meanwhile, water parks can be built on the water surface, promoting marine tourism development.
The construction of cross-sea bridges not only shortens the distance between islands and the mainland but also facilitates regional economic integration.

In the water volume, vertical aquaculture can significantly enhance the comprehensive utilization efficiency of waterbodies while reducing the impact on the ecological environment. On the seabed, the subsea cable and pipelines provide essential connections of energy and information for distant islands and offshore facilities. Meanwhile, the tunnels in the subsoil closely connect the islands, enabling rapid transportation between them.

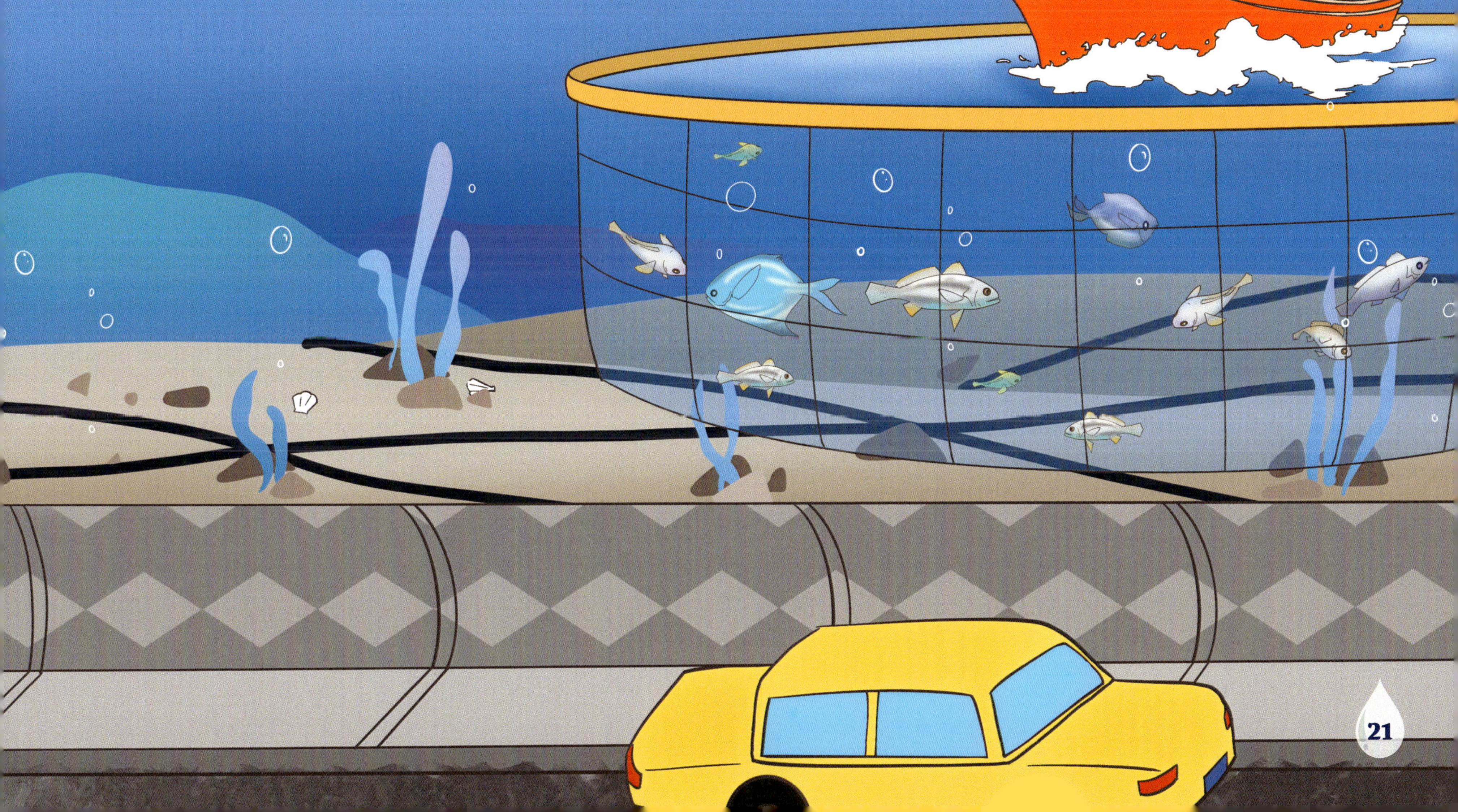

Currently, Zhejiang Province has already implemented vertical management in 3,400 hectares of marine areas. And this is just the beginning.

The jurisdictional sea area of Zhejiang Province is approximately 44,000 square kilometers. In an ideal situation, if each layer of its sea area is fully utilized, it would be equivalent to having an extra land area of Zhejiang, drastically enhancing the efficiency of spatial resource use.

The vertical utilization and high-level protection of marine resources is a systematic project. From a "two-dimensional" ocean to a "three-dimensional" ocean, Zhejiang has taken a solid step forward in this field.

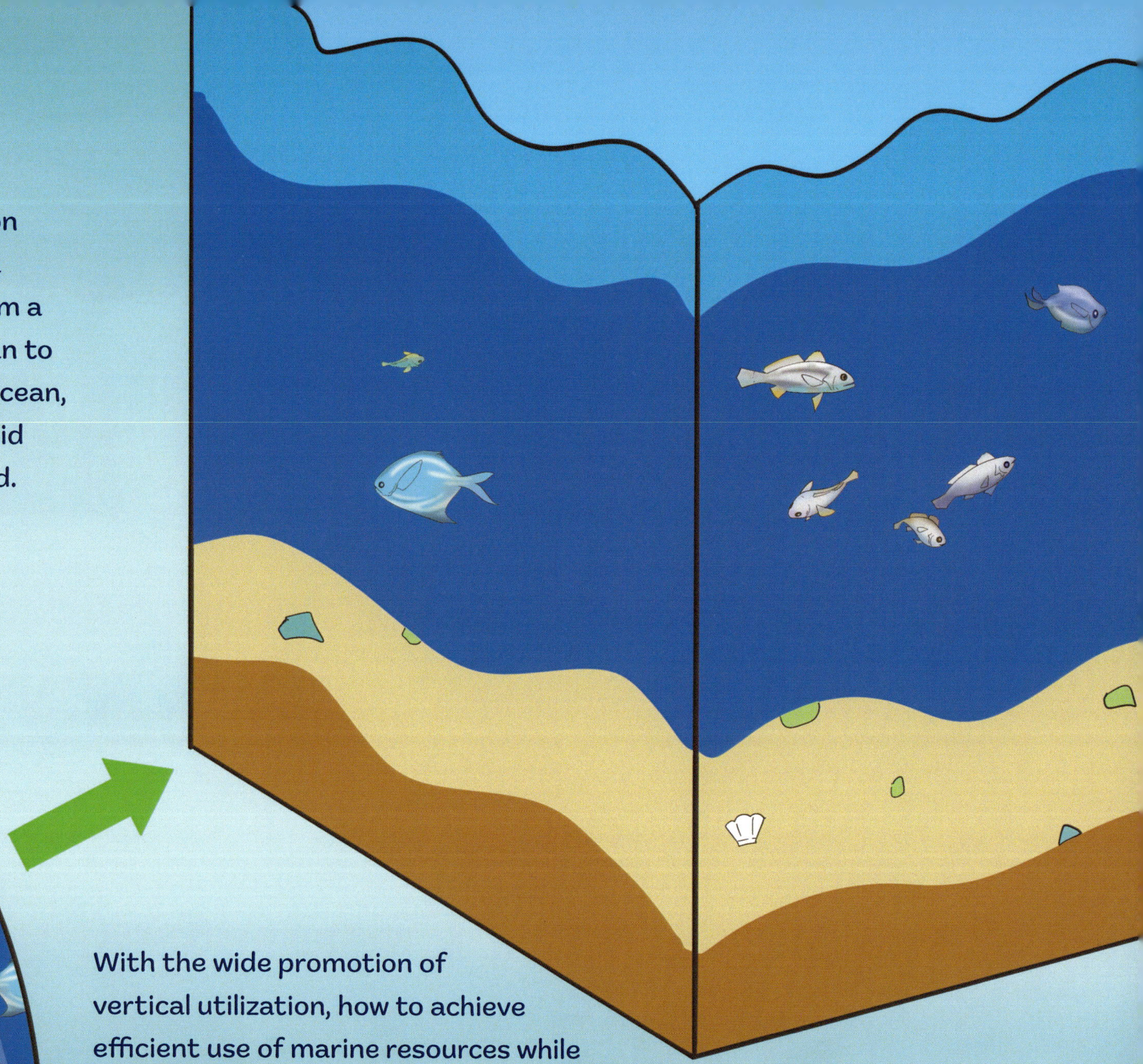

With the wide promotion of vertical utilization, how to achieve efficient use of marine resources while ensuring high-level protection will become a long-term focus and effort for us.

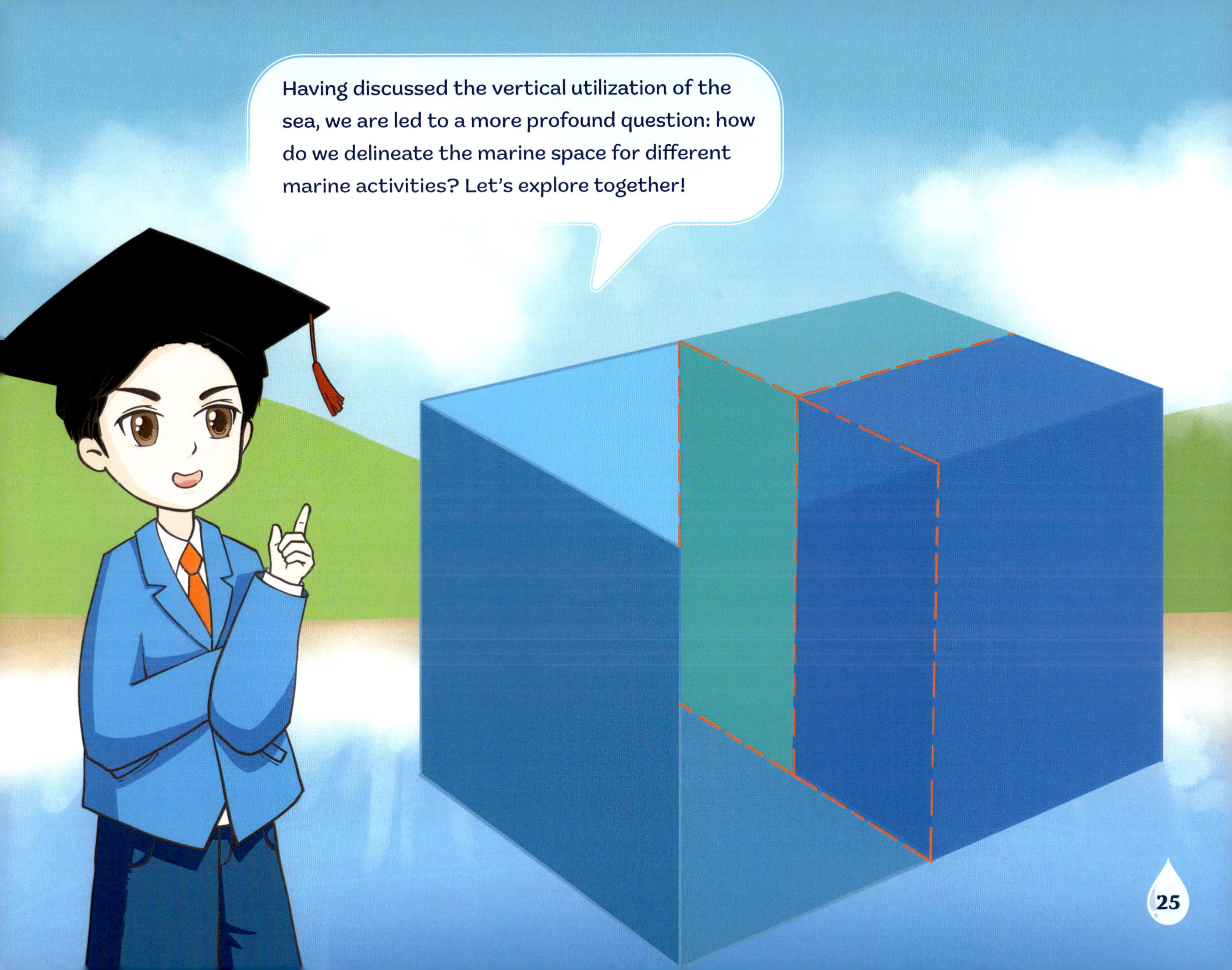
Having discussed the vertical utilization of the sea, we are led to a more profound question: how do we delineate the marine space for different marine activities? Let's explore together!

Based on the four-layer marine space, we can categorize the marine spaces primarily into two types of usage demands and characteristics: operation space and occupied space.

1 Operation space refers to the marine area where the main project of a marine activity is located or the primary marine space used for marine activities. This space is the most direct, fundamental, and important space for marine development and utilization. It is divided into layers: surface, water volume, seabed and subsoil. The operation space is exclusive, ensuring that marine activities can proceed smoothly.

2 Occupied space refers to other spaces occupied by marine engineering projects due to their physical properties and spaces required for periodic maintenance. Within appropriate limits, occupied space can be shared with other marine activities.

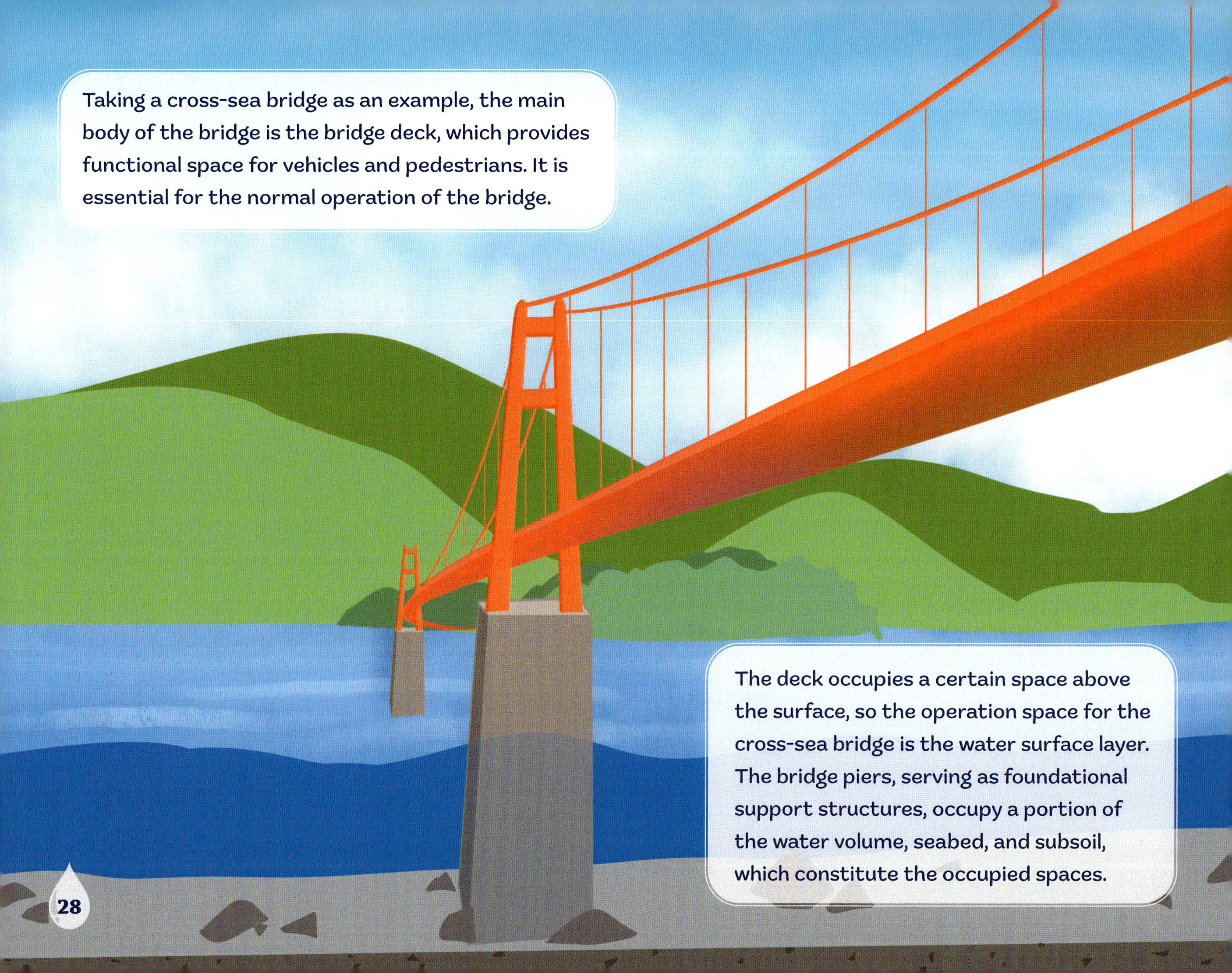

Taking a cross-sea bridge as an example, the main body of the bridge is the bridge deck, which provides functional space for vehicles and pedestrians. It is essential for the normal operation of the bridge.

The deck occupies a certain space above the surface, so the operation space for the cross-sea bridge is the water surface layer. The bridge piers, serving as foundational support structures, occupy a portion of the water volume, seabed, and subsoil, which constitute the occupied spaces.

Taking port basins and navigation channels as another example, passing ships are the primary users of marine space, occupying a certain space above the water surface. Therefore, the water surface is the operation space for port basins and navigation channels.

Additionally, a portion of the ship is submerged in the upper water volume, so this part of the water volume is the occupied space. Moreover, to meet the depth requirements for normal ship navigation, port basins and navigation channels need to be regularly dredged. Therefore, this portion of the seabed and subsoil is considered occupied space required for maintenance.

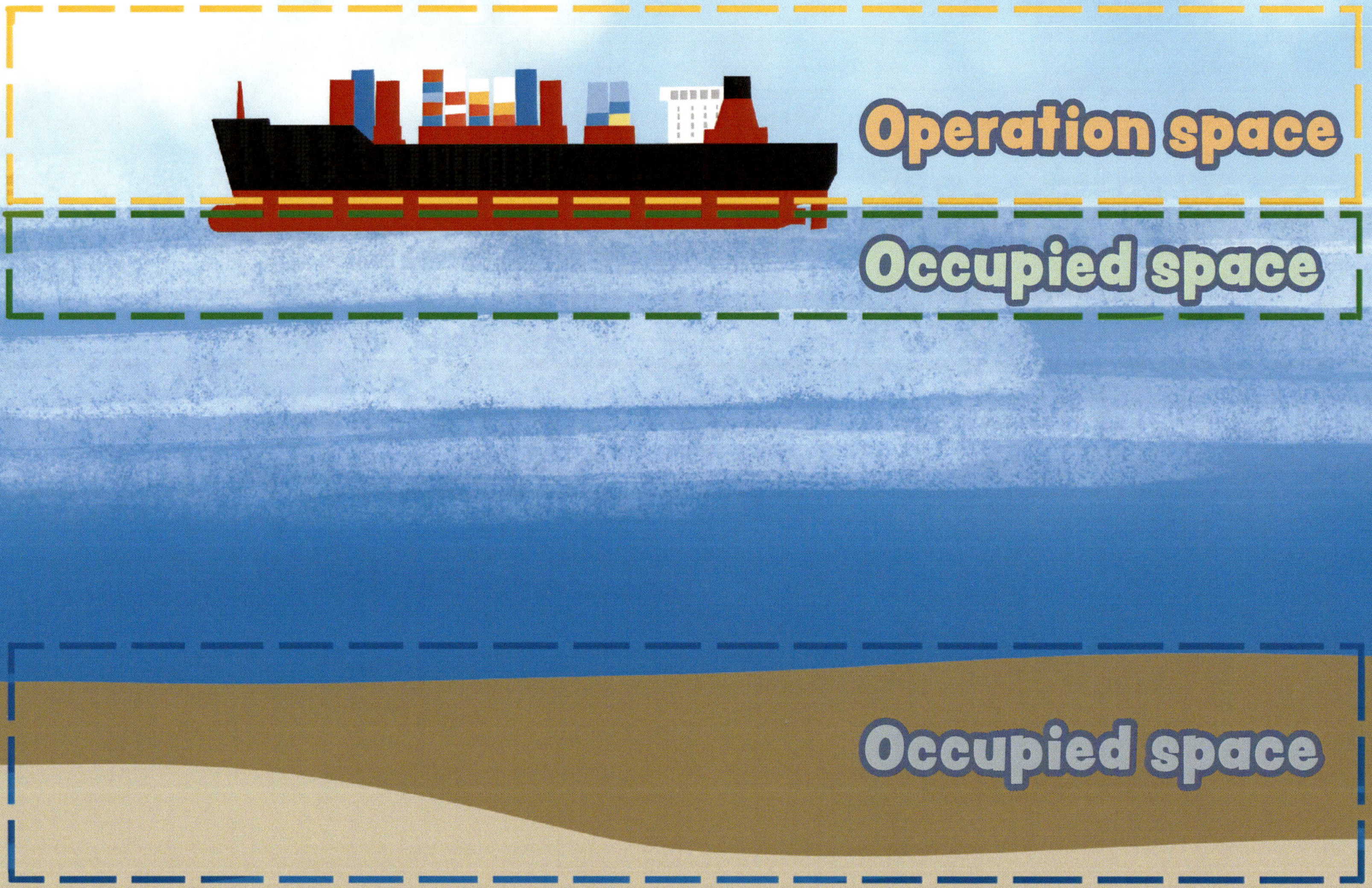

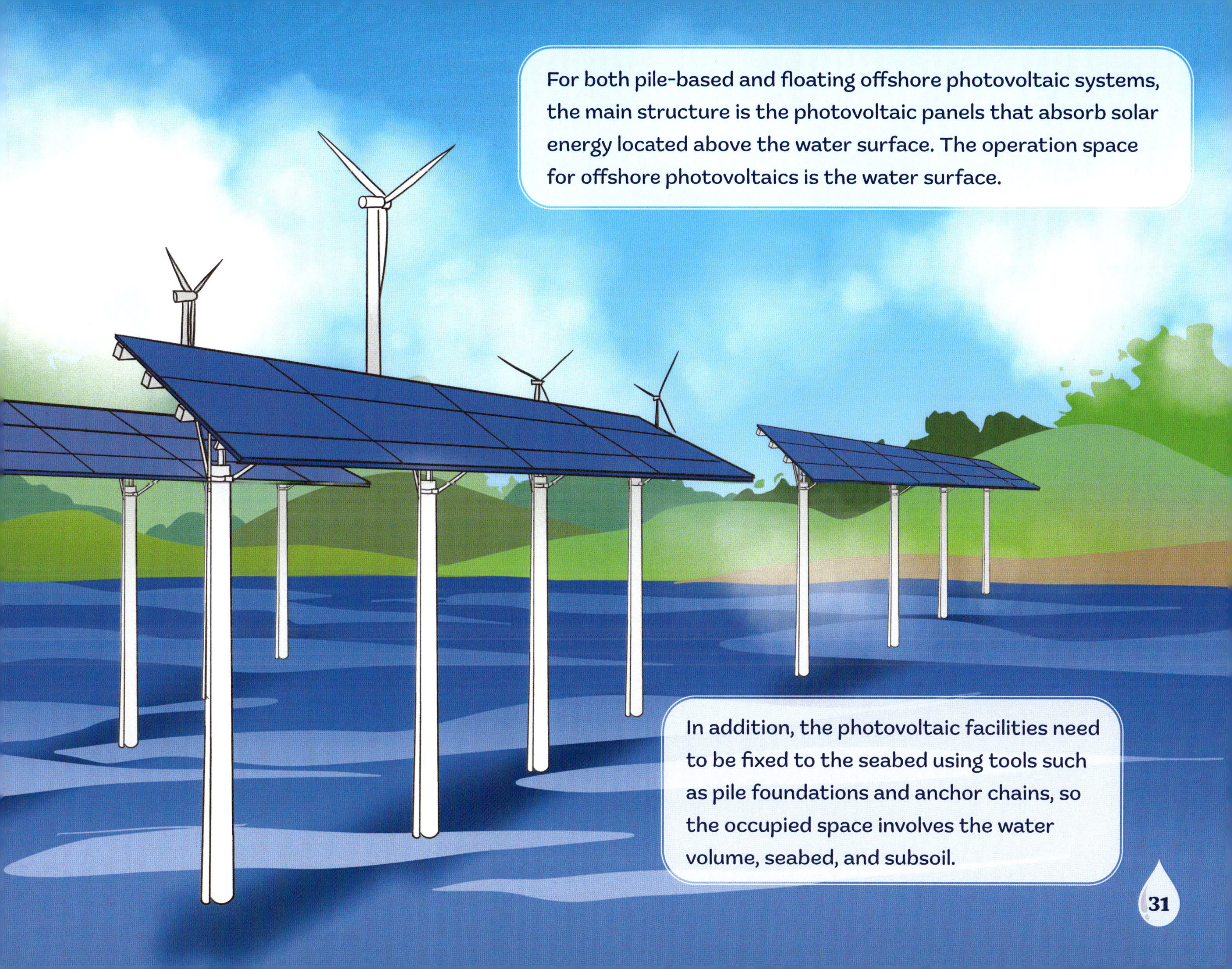

For both pile-based and floating offshore photovoltaic systems, the main structure is the photovoltaic panels that absorb solar energy located above the water surface. The operation space for offshore photovoltaics is the water surface.

In addition, the photovoltaic facilities need to be fixed to the seabed using tools such as pile foundations and anchor chains, so the occupied space involves the water volume, seabed, and subsoil.

For submarine cable pipelines, depending on the construction technique, the operation space for seabed-laid cables is the seabed. For those cables buried in the subsoil, their primary layer of maritime space utilized is the subsoil.

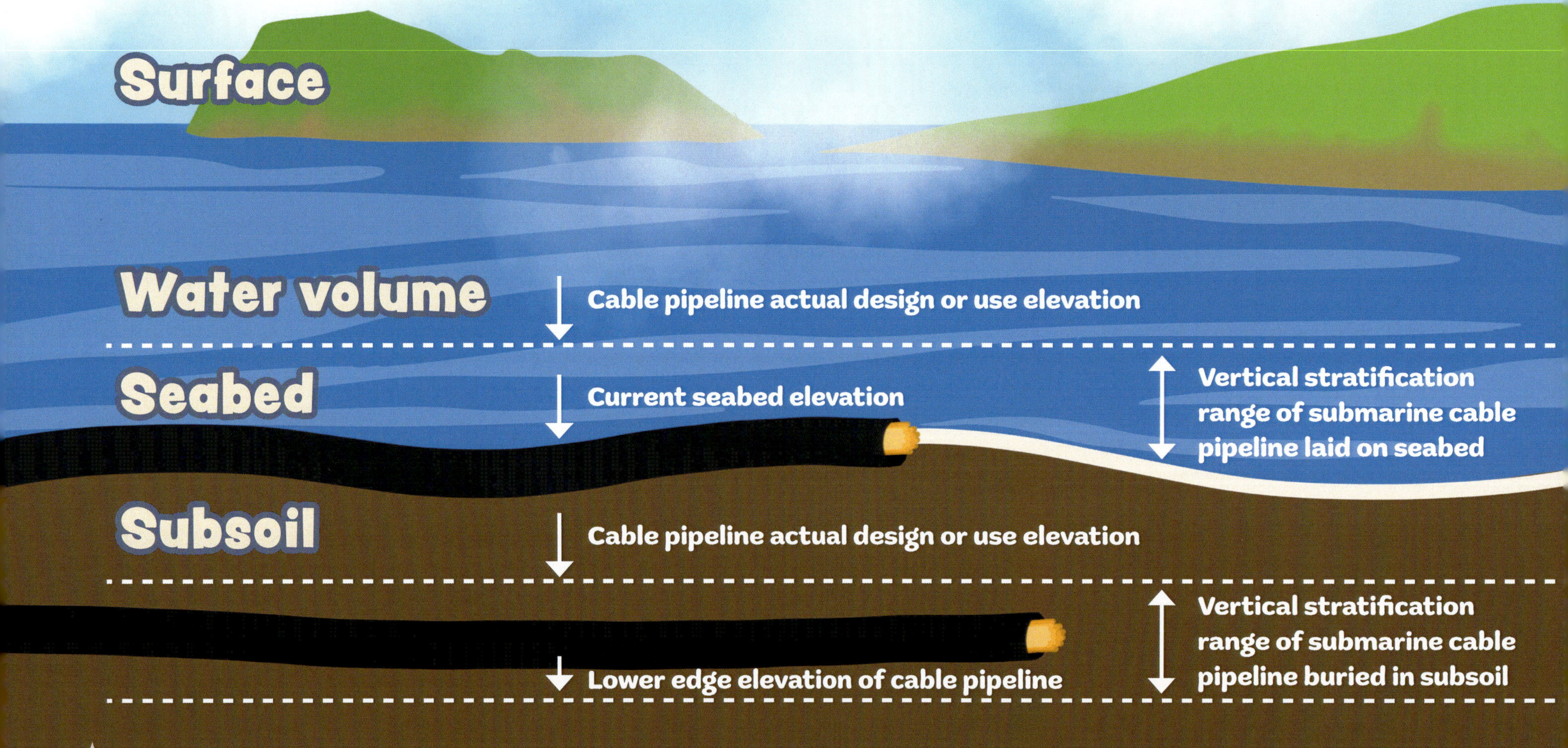

For marine aquaculture, enclosed sea farming and open-water cultivation farming, such as raft and cage culture, the primary marine space utilized is the water volume.

Cage culture, for instance, is the most prevalent method for the cultivation of large yellow croaker.

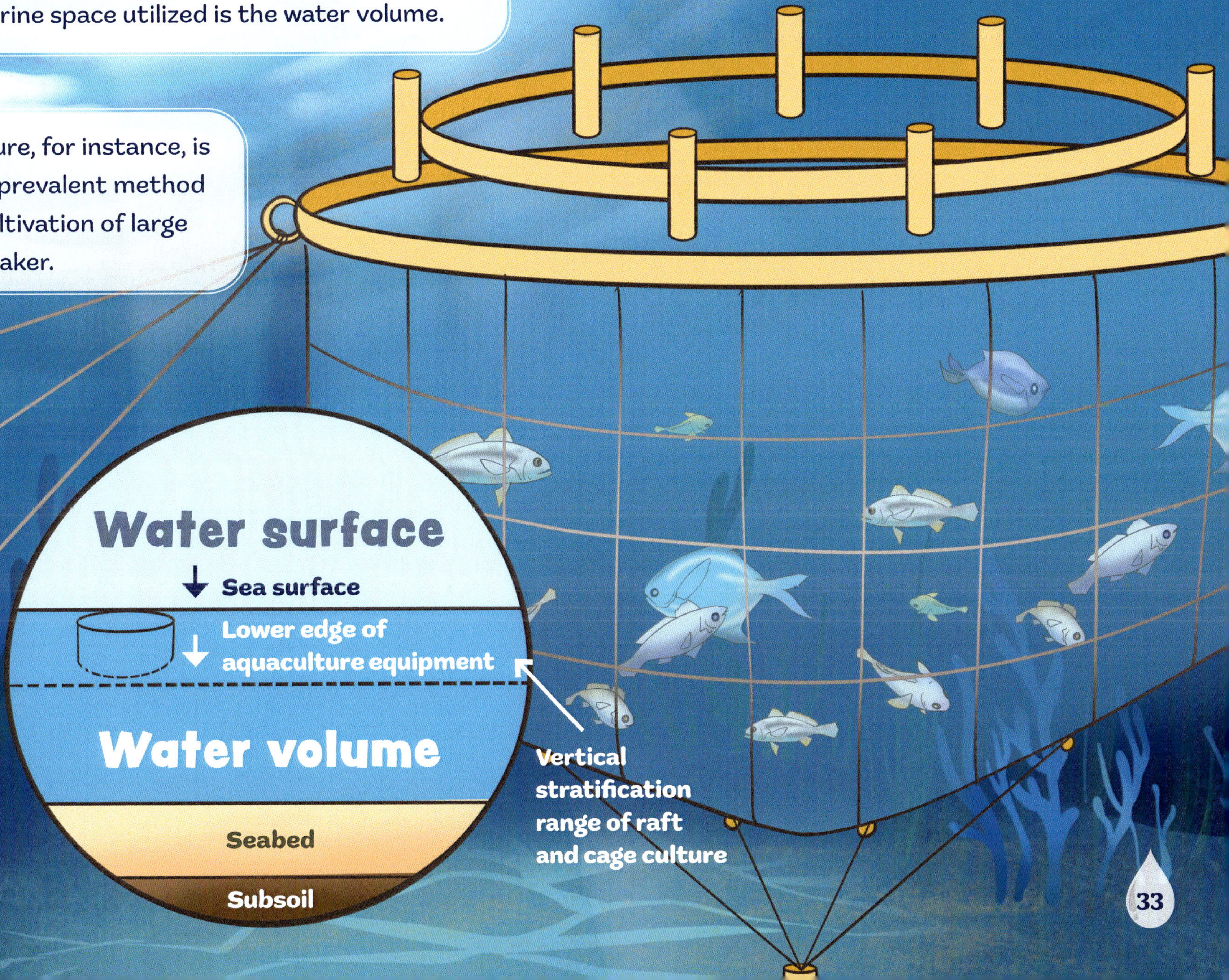

For bottom-culture aquaculture involving manual seeding on the seabed and artificial fish reefs constructed by sunken ships, rock piles, and man-made blocks in the sea, the primary marine space utilized is the seabed. Commonly cultivated species include sea cucumbers, shellfish (such as oysters, clams, and razor clams), and others.

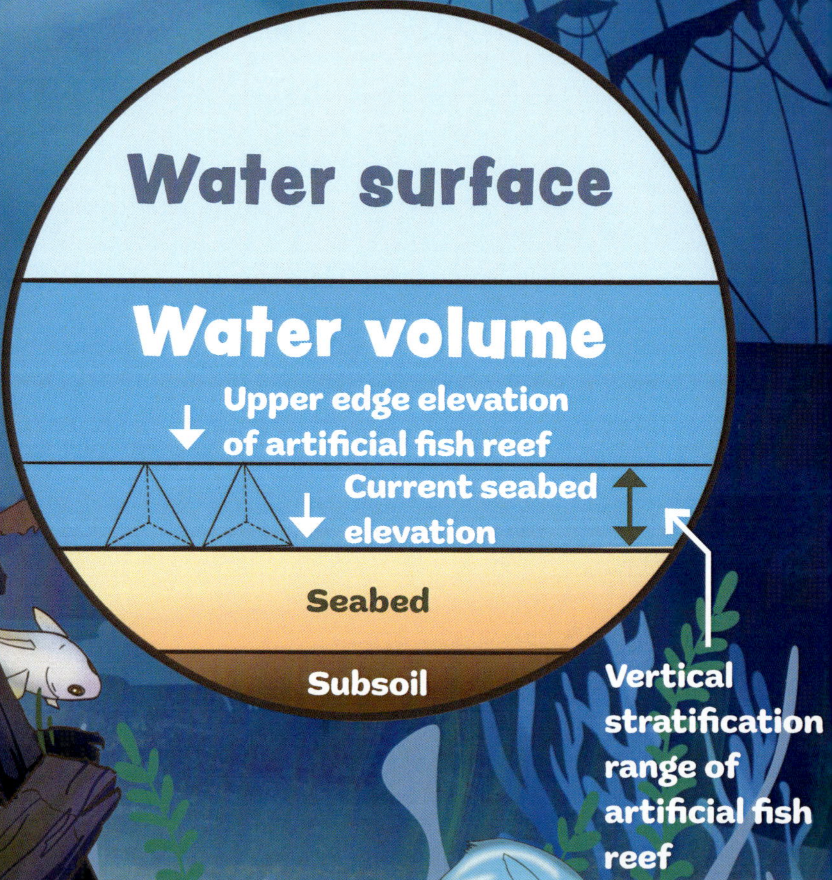

What are some other typical and distinctive combinations of vertically stratified utilization of its marine spaces?

Zhejiang, which follows the principle of "living by the sea, earning from the sea, and thinking about the sea's potential," boasts more than just the typical combination of cross-sea bridges and aquaculture in its marine spatial utilization.

To actively reduce carbon emissions and promote the sustainable development of offshore renewable energy, cities like Ningbo, Wenzhou, Jiaxing, Zhoushan, and Taizhou have begun exploring a "fishery-photovoltaic complementary" power generation model.

Case Study 1
Fishery-Photovoltaic Complementary Model

Install photovoltaic panels above the water surface for power generation and allow fish and shrimp farming in the water below. The photovoltaic arrays can also provide good shading for the fish, creating a new model of vertically integrated utilization where the upper layer generates electricity while the lower layer supports fish farming.

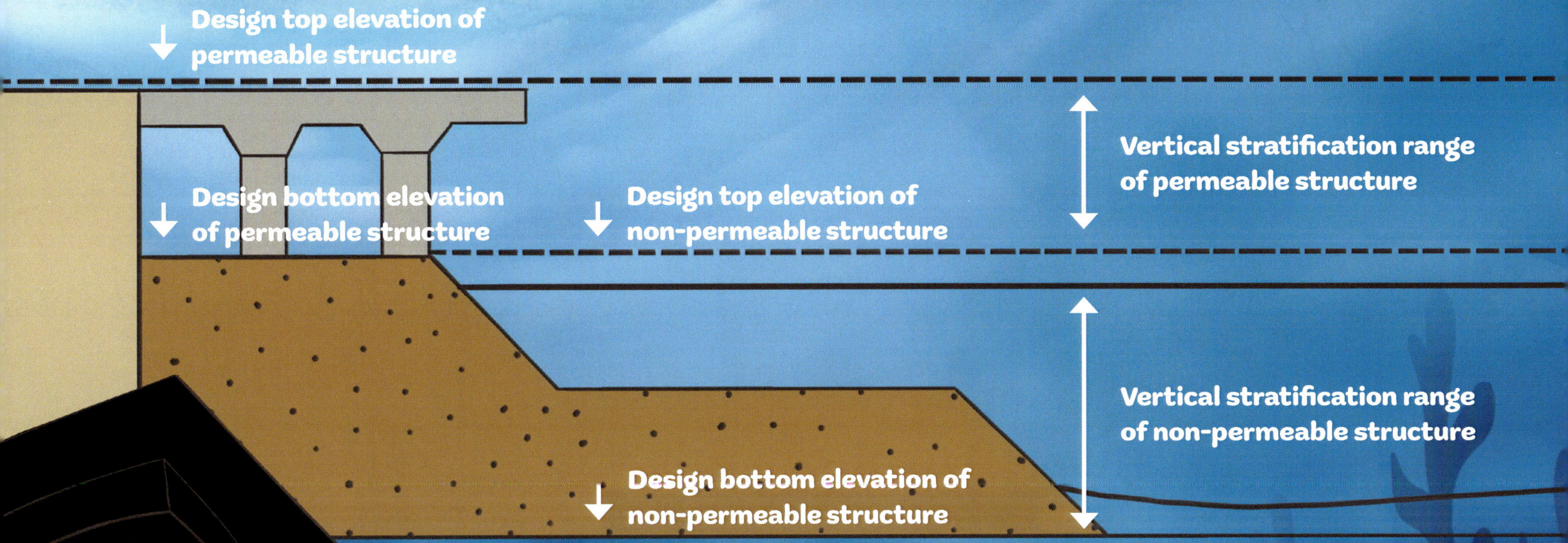

In 2020, Zhejiang Province launched the Coastal Embankment Security Project, which aims to explore new pathways for ecological seawall construction. In this process, seawalls were endowed with multiple functions, including safety protection, industrial development, scenic tourism, ecological coastline preservation, and thematic cultural representations.

In Yueqing, Zhejiang, a permeable structure was used to create a waterfront platform atop the seawall stabilization layers.

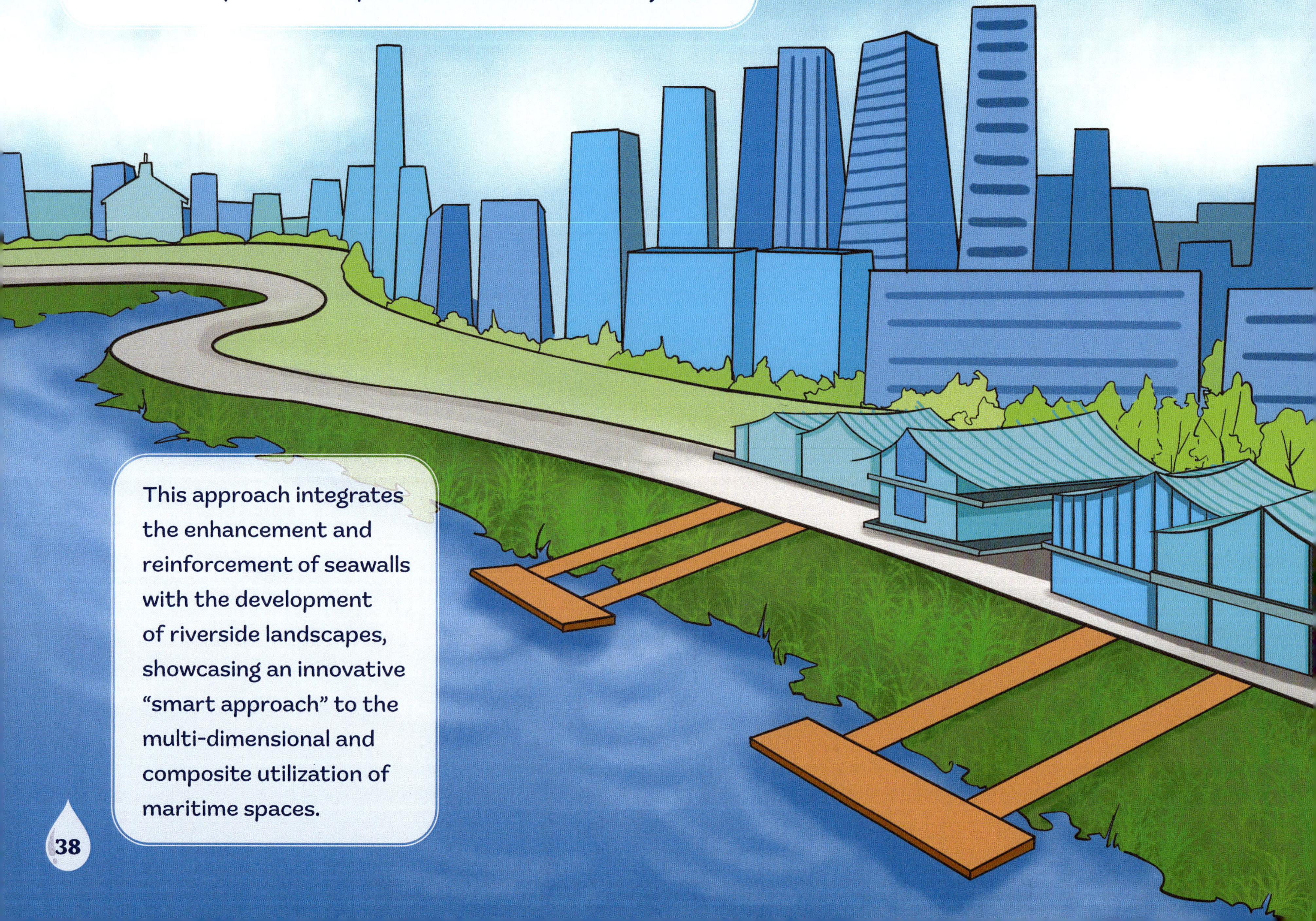

This approach integrates the enhancement and reinforcement of seawalls with the development of riverside landscapes, showcasing an innovative “smart approach” to the multi-dimensional and composite utilization of maritime spaces.

Case Study 3

Dock + Submarine Cables

Submarine cables play a crucial role in ocean communication, power transmission, and chemical transport. These long linear projects often encounter issues related to overlapping marine utilization. In the Jiaxing Port Area of Zhejiang, two chemical submarine pipelines crossing seven docks were constructed by sharing the subsoil space layer while ensuring the safety of the 10,000-ton berth at the dock. The successful construction of submarine pipelines has supported the integrated development of industries in the Jiaxing Port Area.

About the Authors

Wang Peng

Senior Engineer, Postdoctoral Fellow, and Deputy Director of Marine Academy of Zhejiang Province. He serves as a special expert for the Financial and Economic Committee of the Zhejiang Provincial People's Congress and is recognized as a Zhejiang Provincial Science and Technology Expert. In the past five years, he has published over forty academic papers, authored six scholarly works, and received several awards, including a Zhejiang Science and Technology Progress Award, three National Marine Engineering Science and Technology Awards, and a National Geographic Information Science and Technology Progress Award.

Wu Jiexuan

Master's degree in Cartography and Geographic Information Systems, Senior Engineer. She has extensive experience in researching the property rights system of marine resource assets.